RISING STARS

BRAIN ACADEMY
MATHS CHALLENGES

CW00446999

Mission
File
2

Ages
7-8

Published in Association with

nace
National Association
for Able Children in Education

Rising Stars are grateful to the following people for their support in developing this series: Sue Mordecai, Julie Fitzpatrick, Johanna Raffan and Belle Wallace.

NACE, The Core Business Centre, Milton Hill, Abingdon, Oxon OX13 6AB
www.nace.co.uk

RISING STARS

Rising Stars Ltd, 7 Hatchers Mews, Bermondsey Street, London SE1 3GS
www.risingstars-uk.com

Every effort has been made to trace copyright holders and obtain their permission for the use of copyright materials. The authors and publisher will gladly receive information enabling them to rectify any error or omission in subsequent editions.

All facts are correct at time of going to press.

First edition published 2004
This edition published 2011

Text, design and layout © Rising Stars UK Ltd.
TASC: Thinking Actively in a Social Context © Belle Wallace 2004

Written by: Charlotte Haggis, Louise Moore and Richard Cooper
Editorial consultants: Elaine Sellars, Sue Lowndes and Sally Harbour
Design: Burville-Riley
Illustrations: Cover and insides – Sue Lee / Characters – Bill Greenhead
Cover design: Burville-Riley Partnership

All rights reserved. No part of this publication may be reproduced, stored in a retrieval system, or transmitted, in any form by any means, electronic, mechanical, photocopying, recording or otherwise, without the prior permission of Rising Stars.

British Library Cataloguing in Publication Data
A CIP record for this book is available from the British Library.

ISBN (Trade): 978-1-84680-884-5
ISBN (Schools): 978-1-84680-899-9

Printed by Craft Print International Ltd.

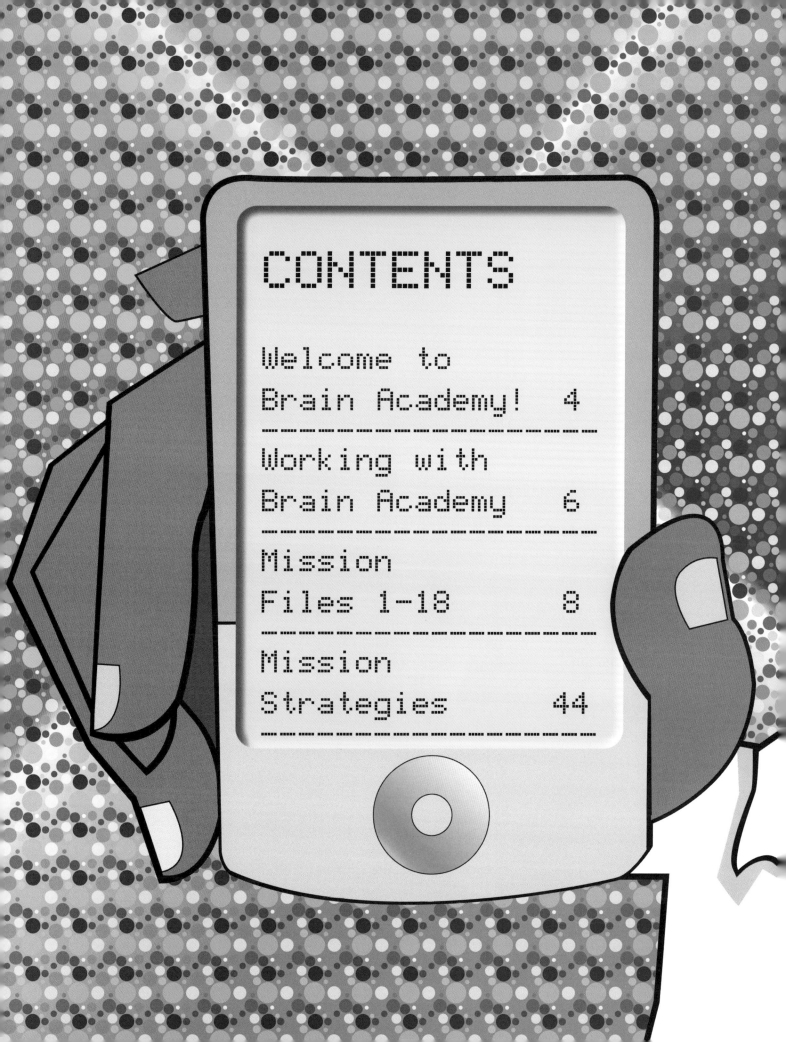

CONTENTS

Welcome to Brain Academy!

Welcome to Brain Academy! Make yourself at home. We are here to give you the low-down on the organisation – so pay attention!

It's our job to help Da Vinci and his colleagues to solve the tough problems they face and we would like you to join us as members of the Academy. Are you up to the challenge?

Da Vinci

Da Vinci is the founder and head of the Brain Academy. He is all seeing, all thinking and all knowing – possibly the cleverest person alive. Nobody has ever actually seen him in the flesh as he communicates only via computer. When Da Vinci receives an emergency call for help, the members of Brain Academy jump into action (and that means you!).

Huxley

Huxley is Da Vinci's right-hand man. Not as clever, but still very smart. He is here to guide you through the missions and offer help and advice. The sensible and reliable face of Brain Academy, Huxley is cool under pressure.

Dr Hood

The mad doctor is the arch-enemy of Da Vinci and Brain Academy. He has set up a rival organisation called D.A.F.T. (which stands for Dull And Feeble Thinkers). Dr Hood and his agents will do anything they can to irritate and annoy the good people of this planet. He is a pain we could do without.

Hilary Kumar

Ms Kumar is the Prime Minister of our country. As the national leader she has a hotline through to the Academy but will only call in an extreme emergency. Confident and strong willed, she is a very tough cookie indeed.

General Cods-Wallop

This highly decorated gentleman (with medals, not wallpaper) is in charge of the armed forces. Most of his success has come from the help of Da Vinci and the Academy rather than the use of his somewhat limited military brain.

Mrs Tiggles

Stella Tiggles is the retired head of the Secret Intelligence service. She is a particular favourite of Da Vinci who treats her as his own mother. Mrs Tiggles' faithful companion is her cat, Bond… James Bond.

We were just like you once – ordinary schoolchildren leading ordinary lives. Then one day we all received a call from a strange character named Da Vinci. From that day on, we have led a double life – as secret members of Brain Academy!

Here are a few things you should know about the people you'll meet on your journey.

Maryland T. Wordsworth
M.T. Wordsworth is the president of the USA. Not the sharpest tool in the box, Maryland prefers to be known by his middle name, Texas, or 'Tex' for short. He takes great exception to being referred to as 'Mary' (which has happened in the past).

Buster Crimes
Buster is a really smooth dude and is in charge of the Police Force. His laid-back but efficient style has won him many friends, although these don't include Dr Hood or the agents of D.A.F.T. who regularly try to trick the coolest cop in town.

Sandy Buckett
The fearless Sandy Buckett is the head of the fire service. Sandy and her team of brave firefighters are always on hand, whether to extinguish the flames of chaos caused by the demented Dr Hood or just to rescue Mrs Tiggles' cat…

Echo the Eco-Warrior
Echo is the hippest chick around. Her love of nature and desire for justice will see her do anything to help an environmental cause – even if it means she's going to get her clothes dirty.

Victor Blastov
Victor Blastov is the leading scientist at the Space Agency. He once tried to build a rocket by himself but failed to get the lid off the glue. Victor often requires the services of the Academy, even if it's to set the video to record Dr Who.

Prince Barrington
Prince Barrington, or 'Bazza' as he is known to his friends, is the publicity-seeking heir to the throne. Always game for a laugh, the Prince will stop at nothing to raise money for worthy causes. A 'good egg' as his mother might say.

Working with Brain Academy

Do you get the idea? Now you've had the introduction we are going to show you the best way to use this book.

The plot

This tells you what the mission is about.

MISSION FILE 2:16

Echo is no birdbrain!

tri   quad   bi   uni

Time: Just after lunch
Place: A park in South London

A flock of South American Fluffy-Nuts has escaped from the 'American National Zoo' and headed straight for England. Each bird has its own unique colour of crest feathers. Echo has agreed to help return these rare and beautiful birds. She needs to call Brain Academy...

Da Vinci? What must I do?

Get your coat and get ready for your training mission with Huxley

The Training Mission

Huxley will give you some practice before sending you on the main mission.

TM

OK Echo. First you must take photographs of the birds so that the zookeeper can identify them.

1) In the first phototograph there are five different crest feathers. Which birds could have been in the photograph?

2) How many possible answers can you find?

38

Each mission is divided up into different parts.

No one said this was easy. In fact that is why you have been chosen. Da Vinci will only take the best and he believes that includes you. Good luck!

Each book contains a number of 'missions' for you to take part in. You will work with the characters in Brain Academy to complete these missions.

The Main Mission

This is where you try to complete the challenge.

M1

Echo needs to take photographs of all the birds to send to the zookeeper. Answer these questions and he'll be sure to recognise them.

1) In the next photograph there are six different crest feathers. Which birds could be in the photograph?

2) How many different answers can you find?

Fantastic! The zookeeper has identified his birds. If Echo can take the Da Vinci Challenge she can return them to their home.

The Da Vinci Files

These problems are for the best Brain Academy recruits. Very tough. Are you tough enough?

Da Vinci files

In the next photograph, Echo sees SEVEN different crest feathers. Which birds could be in the photograph?

Huxley's Think Tank

Write the names and number of feathers at the top of your page. Work out sums using the lowest numbers first.

39

Huxley's Think Tank

Huxley will download some useful tips onto your PDA to help you on each mission.

PS: See pages 44–47 for a useful process and hints and tips!

Fund-raising for fire engines!

Time: Time for a cake!
Place: Sandy Buckett's fire station

Sandy Buckett is having a cake sale to raise some money to buy a new fire engine. Prince Barrington has come along to buy some cakes. He's having a few problems counting out his money. He's going to need some help from Brain Academy!

I'm hungry, Da Vinci. Please help me get started!

Huxley has a Training Mission that will have you eating cakes in no time!

Prince Barrington only has 1p, 2p and 5p coins in his pocket. Can you help him to work out how many of each he has so that he can start buying cakes?

1) Prince Barrington has 20p in his pocket. He has 10 coins. Which coins does he have?

2) The Prince has 30p in his pocket. He has 10 coins. Which coins does he have?

3) Prince Barrington has 30p in his pocket. He has 20 coins. Which coins does he have?

M1

Prince Barrington needs to give Sandy the correct money for each cake. Can you help him to pay for these cakes using the correct money?

1) Prince Barrington buys a cake for 6p. He pays for it with the exact amount of money. What combination of coins can he use?

2) How many different combinations of coins can the Prince use to make 6p?

3) How many different ways can the Prince pay for an 8p cake using the exact amount of money?

4) How many different ways can the Prince pay for a 10p cake using the exact amount of money?

Excellent work! If the Prince can take the Da Vinci challenge, he'll be able to buy enough cakes to last him the rest of the day and Sandy will be on her way to buying her new fire engine.

Da Vinci Files

The Prince paid for a tasty cream cake. He handed over TWO coins and received 1p change. How much did the cake cost? How many possible answers can you find?

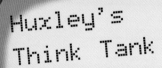

Huxley's Think Tank

Find all the ways to make the total using the lowest possible amount first, e.g:

5p=1p+1p+1p+1p+1p
5p=1p+1p+1p+2p

9

A gem of a challenge!

Time: Late afternoon
Place: Prince Bazza's mansion

Prince Barrington is making a necklace as a present for the Queen to celebrate her birthday. He has bought some beads to thread on to string. The Prince is having a bit of trouble deciding which colour beads to thread. Time to call Brain Academy!

I'm having a string of problems with these beads!

Go and see Huxley. He'll know what to do.

The Prince has FOUR beads. TWO are RED and TWO are BLUE.

1) How many different ways can he thread the FOUR beads on a piece of string?

2) Which patterns are symmetrical?

The Prince has decided to buy some more beads to make this necklace really colourful. He is going to need some help from you to thread the beads.

He has FIVE beads altogether. FOUR are RED and ONE is BLUE.

1) How many different ways are there that he can thread them on the string?

2) How many of these designs are symmetrical?

3) If he has SIX beads altogether and TWO are RED and FOUR are BLUE, show the different symmetrical patterns he could make.

4) Next, he takes SEVEN beads. THREE are RED and FOUR are BLUE. Show the different symmetrical patterns he could make now.

Completing the Da Vinci Challenge will mean that the Prince will be able to wrap up a beautiful necklace to give to the Queen.

Da Vinci files

What if the Prince had bought some GREEN beads as well? Try arranging TWO GREEN beads, TWO RED beads and TWO BLUE beads.

How many symmetrical patterns could he make now?

Huxley's Think Tank

Be sure to record your ideas carefully. Try using letters to stand for the colours to help you do this.

11

A close call!

Time: Mid-afternoon
Place: A pet shop car park

Mrs Tiggles is out shopping with James Bond when she thinks she sees a UFO hovering over the 'Pets 'R' Us' car park. She knows this is a job for Brain Academy...

I must keep this short Da Vinci... **HELP!**

Can't hear you Stella... (crackle) bad line. Call Cods-Wallop direct.

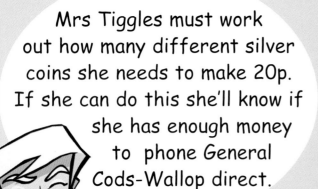

Mrs Tiggles must work out how many different silver coins she needs to make 20p. If she can do this she'll know if she has enough money to phone General Cods-Wallop direct.

1) What is the least number of silver coins Mrs Tiggles will need to make 20p?

2) What is the greatest number of silver coins that Mrs Tiggles will need to make 20p?

3) How many other ways can she make 20p using only silver coins?

5p   10p   20p   50p

5p 10p 20p 50p

Mrs Tiggles has just enough money to phone the army and the air force, and prevent alien invasion. Can you help her do this by answering these questions?

1) The first call costs her 30p. She uses the exact money and she only uses silver coins.
   a) How could she pay for the call?
   b) How many possible answers are there?

2) The second call costs her 40p. Again, she uses the exact money and she only uses silver coins.
   a) How could she pay for the call?
   b) How many possible ways are there for her to do this?

Great work! Mrs Tiggles has made the phone calls to save the world. The old lady and her cat can now get the bus back home... if only she had some change!

Da Vinci files

Mrs Tiggles needs to pay for James to get on the bus. His fare is 20p and the driver will only take the exact amount. Using 1p, 2p and 5p coins, how many different ways can you find to pay for the ticket?

Huxley's Think Tank

You can try drawing yourself a table that could be ticked to record your ideas.

5p 10p 20p

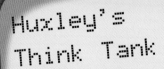

Flower power!

Time: Elevenses
Place: A florist

America is in a sorry state due to the fact that their President is down in the dumps! Until he feels happier, he just won't be able to run the country properly. Hilary Kumar has agreed to help America by cheering up her old pal!

America needs us to cheer up Tex. Where do we start, Da Vinci?

Grab your joke book and jump on the first plane to America. But don't forget to do Huxley's Training Mission first!

Red and white flowers are just what Tex needs to get rid of those grumps. Can you help Hilary to cheer her pal up by choosing some?

1) Hilary buys THREE bunches of flowers. How many bunches of each colour could she take to Tex?

2) Hilary buys FOUR bunches of flowers. What combinations of bunches could she take to Tex?

14

If Hilary is going to put a smile on Tex's face she needs to buy a few more flowers. Can you help her?

1) What if Hilary bought SEVEN bunches? Again she chooses red or white ones. What combinations of flowers could she take to Tex?

2) If there are ELEVEN possible ways that Hilary could buy red and white ones, how many plants did she buy?

Excellent work! Hilary's flowers are sure to cheer Tex up. Now she'd like to buy some more flowers to say 'thank you' to everyone who has helped her.

Da Vinci files

Hilary quite likes the blue flowers too. She buys THREE bunches of either red, white or blue. How many combinations of flowers could she buy?

Huxley's Think Tank

You could use red, white and blue counters to stand for the flowers. Try writing a letter to stand for each colour e.g. R W B

Legs everywhere!

Time: Dawn
Place: Outside a toy shop

Buster Crimes, head of the police, is chasing some D.A.F.T. agents who have stolen a sack of whoopee cushions from a toyshop. These crooks are breaking wind and breaking the law and they must be stopped! Can you help Buster?

TOY SHOP

The bottom line is that these thieves must be caught. Da Vinci, please help!

Pop along and see Huxley. He has a Training Mission that should help you.

TM

To pass the Training Mission you will need to work out how many officers arrived to help Buster.

There was at least one police officer and one police dog that came to help. Altogether there were 20 legs.

How many police dogs and officers could there be at the scene of the crime? There are FOUR different answers. Can you find them all?

Answering these questions will mean that some of the thieves can be caught.

There was at least one police officer and one police dog that came to help. Altogether there were 28 legs.

1) How many police dogs and officers could there be at the scene of the crime? There are SIX different answers. How many can you find?

More officers kept arriving to lend a hand. At the next count there were 36 legs. There were 14 heads.

2) How many police dogs and officers could there be at the scene of the crime?

Completing the Da Vinci Challenge will mean that these whoopee cushion thieves will be put 'behind' bars for a very long time.

Da Vinci files

At the final count there were a total of 40 legs. Explore how many officers and how many dogs could have been at the scene of the crime. Don't forget, there is at least ONE of each.

Huxley's Think Tank

You'll need to practise counting in FOURs and counting in TWOs. Using different coloured cubes to represent the officers and dogs may help.

Target practice!

Time: Midday
Place: British Army summer fête

It is the day of the British Army Summer Fête. General Cods-Wallop has decided that he wants to win some prizes to donate to his local hospital. He has decided to try his luck at archery.

I'm 'aiming' for a top score, Da Vinci. Can you help me?

Huxley's Training Mission is the place to start.

Can you help General Cods-Wallop reach his target of getting a top score with his THREE arrows. Answering these questions will win a prize for the local hospital.

1) What is the highest score that General Harvey Cods-Wallop can get with THREE arrows?

2) Can you find all the different ways he can score a total of NINE if all THREE arrows hit the target?

Answering these questions will mean that Harvey can win a whole tankful of goodies to donate to the hospital. He's going to need your help to do it though.

1) How many ways are there that he can get a score of 10 with THREE arrows?

2) What is the highest score that Harvey Cods-Wallop can get with FOUR arrows?

3) How many ways can he score a total of 10 with FOUR arrows if they all hit the target?

Spot on! Help the General to win the star prize by completing the Da Vinci Challenge.

Da Vinci files

How many other scores can you find that the General can score with THREE arrows?

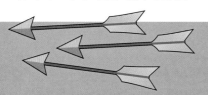

Huxley's Think Tank

Think carefully about how you record your work.
He can hit the same number more than once.

A mountain of a problem

Time: Mid-morning
Place: Mount Eveready

Mountain climber Ivor Problem is in trouble. He is lost on Mount Eveready! General Cods-Wallop has set off to find him. He puts a bar of chocolate and some woolly jumpers in his backpack, as he knows Ivor will be cold and hungry when he finds him.

Will you help me save this chap, Da Vinci?

Huxley's Training Mission will set you on the right path!

To complete your Training Mission you must decide how many ways TWO people can share these woolly jumpers. It's freezing up there so you'd better get it right!

1) How many ways can TWO people share FOUR jumpers?

2) How many ways can TWO people share FIVE jumpers?

3) Continue investigating sharing jumpers between TWO people.

Keep a track of your answers. You could use a table to do this. You may be able to notice some patterns.

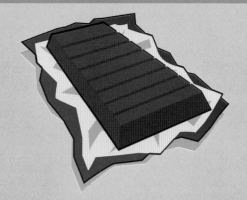

M1

When the General finds Ivor Problem, he is very hungry. Can you help General Cods-Wallop by working out how the TWO men can share the EIGHT-piece bar of chocolate?

1) Investigate all the different ways that General Harvey Cods–Wollop can share the EIGHT-piece bar between TWO people. The pieces don't have to be the same size.

2) Ivor Problem has a pet mouse in his pocket. How many ways can THREE of them share the chocolate?

Completing the Da Vinci Challenge will mean that the General can save Ivor Problem and his pets.

Da Vinci files

A passing, hungry mountain goat would like some chocolate too. Ivor needs to eat the most chocolate. What different ways are there of sharing out the chocolate bar between the FOUR making sure that Ivor has the most?

Huxley's Think Tank

Make yourself a pretend chocolate bar with multi-link cubes and try breaking it in different ways.

What's the score?

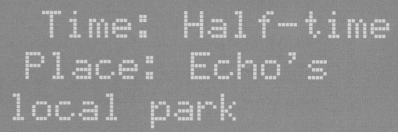

The animal rescue centre is falling apart and there is no money to fix it. Echo the Eco Warrior has organised a charity netball tournament to raise funds. She's having a few problems with the scores though. Time to call Brain Academy.

I just can't keep track of the scores, Da Vinci. Please help!

Huxley will help you achieve your goal, Echo!

TM

OK, Echo, if you can work out how many matches will be played, you'll be able to buy a new roof for the animal rescue centre!

1) If FOUR teams take part in the tournament, how many games could be played?

2) If the matches are played one at a time and each match lasts 20 minutes, how long would it take to play all the matches?

M1

There are THREE matches to play so it's time for the tournament to begin. Answering these questions will mean that the animal rescue centre will be able to afford new doors and windows.

1) The full-time score of the first match was:

   Team A **1**   Team B **2**
   What are all the possible half-time scores?

2) The full-time score of the second match was:

   Team C **2**   Team D **3**
   What are all the possible half-time scores?

3) In the final of the tournament the full-time score was:

   Team B **4**   Team D **1**
   What are all the possible half-time scores?

Excellent! Completing the Da Vinci Challenge will mean that enough money will have been raised for them to buy a brand new gym for the animals.

Da Vinci Files

Prince Barrington said that he would donate £3 to the charity for each goal scored.
If the teams had earned £27 by half-time, what could the possible scores have been?

Huxley's Think Tank

Don't forget that the half-time score can be the same as the full time score.

23

The great train robbery!

Time: Midday
Place: Wombledon Station

Charlie Chugalong is busy building a supersonic train that will travel at record-breaking speed. He needs to get it finished by next Tuesday, but he just can't decide which colour he should paint his terrific train. Victor Blastov has agreed to help solve the problem.

Where should I start, Da Vinci?

Huxley has the perfect 'Train-ing' Mission!

TM

Victor has tins of red paint and tins of blue paint. To pass the Training Mission, Victor must decide how he is going to paint the carriages. Each carriage must be painted using just ONE colour.

1) How many ways are there that Victor can paint TWO carriages using both or either of the tins?

2) How many ways are there that he could paint THREE carriages?

Brain Academy Maths Challenges Mission File 2 Answer booklet

Welcome to Brain Academy Maths! Designed for children who enjoy a challenge, the five Brain Academy books provide a wealth of fun activities and investigations. Suitable for children working at slightly beyond the expected National Curriculum level for their age, all the activities help support the current National Curriculum which can be found at http://curriculum.qcda.gov.uk. Are you and your child ready to become members of Brain Academy? Remember to look at Huxley's Think Tank for a helpful hint when the pressure is on. Good luck!

MISSION FILE 2:1 Fund-raising for fire-engines!

TM Work through these with coins. Pick 10 coins and work out the amount.
If there is too much money, change a large value coin for a smaller value coin. If there isn't enough, change a smaller value coin for a higher value. Repeat until the correct amount is reached.

1) 10 x 2p   or 2 x 5p, 2 x 2p and 6 x 1p
2) 4 x 5p, 4 x 2p and 2 x 1p or 5 x 5p and 5 x 1p
3) 10 x 2p and 10 x 1p   or 2 x 5p, 2 x 2p and 16 x 1p

There may be other solutions – check your child's work.

M1 Where there are lots of possible answers, it's a good idea to draw a table with the values of the coins for support. Remember to exchange coins to find a further answer; if you have an answer involving two 1ps, replace the 1p with a 2p for a different solution.

1) and 2)
1p + 1p + 1p + 1p + 1p + 1p = 6p   2p + 1p + 1p + 1p + 1p = 6p   2p + 2p + 1p + 1p = 6p   5 different ways to pay
2p + 2p + 2p = 6p   5p + 1p = 6p

3) 1p + 1p + 1p + 1p + 1p + 1p + 1p + 1p = 8p   2p + 1p + 1p + 1p + 1p + 1p + 1p = 8p   7 different ways to pay
2p + 2p + 1p + 1p + 1p + 1p = 8p   2p + 2p + 2p + 1p + 1p = 8p   2p + 2p + 2p + 2p = 8p
5p + 2p + 1p = 8p .   5p + 1p + 1p + 1p = 8p

4) 1p + 1p + 1p + 1p + 1p + 1p + 1p + 1p + 1p + 1p = 10p   10 different ways to pay
2p + 1p + 1p + 1p + 1p + 1p + 1p + 1p + 1p = 10p   2p + 2p + 1p + 1p + 1p + 1p + 1p + 1p = 10p
2p + 2p + 2p + 1p + 1p + 1p + 1p = 10p   2p + 2p + 2p + 2p + 1p + 1p = 10p   2p + 2p + 2p + 2p + 2p = 10p
5p + 2p + 2p + 1p = 10p   5p + 2p + 1p + 1p + 1p = 10p   5p + 1p + 1p + 1p + 1p + 1p = 10p   5p + 5p = 10p

Da Vinci files

The only coins that could be handed over where 1p would be change and not return of the money given are:
2 x 5p, 5p + 2p or 2 x 2p.
2 x 5p   change 1p → cake cost 9p   5p + 2p   change 1p → cake cost 6p
2 x 2p   change 1p → cake cost 3p
(3 possible answers)

MISSION FILE 2:2 A gem of a challenge!

Remember, the order matters in this Mission, so RRBB is not the same as BBRR.

TM

1) RRBB, RBRB, RBBR, BRRB, BRBR, BBRR   (6 solutions)
2) RBBR and BRRB are symmetrical.

M1

1) BRRRR, RBRRR, RRBRR, RRRBR, RRRRB   (5 ways)
2) 1 symmetrical design   RRBRR
3) 3 symmetrical designs RBBBBR, BRBBRB, BBRRBB
4) 3 symmetrical designs BBRRRBB, BRBRBRB, RBBRBBR

Da Vinci files

6 symmetrical designs
GBRRBG, GRBBRG, RGBBGR, RBGGBR, BRGGRB, BGRRGB

TM

1) One (20p)
2) 4 x 5p
3) 10p and 10p   10p, 5p and 5p   4 ways altogether (see answers 1) and 2))

M1

1a) Add 5p + 5p + 5p + 5p + 5p + 5p
1b) 6 ways
2a) Add 5p + 5p + 5p + 5p + 5p + 5p + 5p + 5p
2b) 9 ways

Da Vinci files

Remember to exchange coins to find a different way; if you have an answer involving two 1ps, replace the 1ps with a 2p for a different solution.

(29 ways)

1p	2p	5p
20	0	0
18	1	0
16	2	0
15	0	1
14	3	0
13	1	1
12	4	0
11	2	1

1p	2p	5p
10	5	0
10	0	2
9	3	1
8	6	0
8	1	2
7	4	1
6	7	0
6	2	2

1p	2p	5p
5	0	3
5	5	1
4	8	0
4	3	2
3	6	1
3	1	3
2	9	0
2	4	2

1p	2p	5p
1	7	1
1	2	3
0	10	0
0	5	2
0	0	4

TM

1) RRR, RRW, RWW, WWW (4 solutions)
(NB: RRW = RWR = WRR because they are all two bunches of red and one bunch of white, so these count as just one solution)

2) RRRR, RRRW, RRWW, RWWW, WWWW (5 solutions)

M1

1) RRRRRRR, RRRRRRW, RRRRRWW, RRRRWWW, RRRWWWW, RRWWWWW, RWWWWWW, WWWWWWW
(8 solutions)

2) RRRRRRRRRR, RRRRRRRRRW, RRRRRRRRWW, RRRRRRRWWW, RRRRRRWWWW, RRRRRWWWWW,
RRRRWWWWWW, RRRWWWWWWW, RRWWWWWWWW, RWWWWWWWWW, WWWWWWWWWW
10 bunches have 11 solutions, because the number of solutions is always one more than the number of bunches.

Da Vinci files

RRR, RRW, RRB, RWW, RBB, RWB, BBB, BBW, BWW, WWW
(10 combinations)

Use the information that one dog has the same number of legs as two officers to help you.

TM

Officers	8	6	4	2
Dogs	1	2	3	4

M1

1)

Officers	12	10	8	6	4	2
Dogs	1	2	3	4	5	6

2) 4 dogs and 10 officers. Draw a table to help.

© Rising Stars UK Ltd. Brain Academy Maths Challenges MF2 Answer Booklet

Officers	18	16	14	12	10	8	6	4	2
Dogs	1	2	3	4	5	6	7	8	9

MISSION FILE 2:6 — Target practice!

TM

1) 3 x 5 = 15
2) 1, 3, 5   1, 4, 4   2, 3, 4   2, 2, 5   (4 ways)

M1

1) 1, 4, 5   2, 4, 4   2, 3, 5   3, 3, 4   (4 ways)
2) 4 x 5 = 20
3) 1, 1, 3, 5   1, 1, 4, 4   1, 2, 2, 5   1, 2, 3, 4   1, 3, 3, 3   2, 2, 3, 3   2, 2, 2, 4   (7 ways)

Da Vinci files

Scores that can be obtained with 3 arrows are:
3, 4, 5, 6, 7, 8, 9, 10, 11, 12, 13, 14, 15
Some of these scores can be obtained in more than one way.

MISSION FILE 2:7 — A mountain of a problem

TM

1) 4 jumpers = 5 ways

General	0	1	2	3	4
Ivor	4	3	2	1	0

2) 5 jumpers = 6 ways

General	0	1	2	3	4	5
Ivor	5	4	3	2	1	0

3) 2 jumpers = 3 ways

General	0	1	2
Ivor	2	1	0

3 jumpers = 4 ways

General	0	1	2	3
Ivor	3	2	1	0

NB: Your child may choose not to record both combinations for a particular split, e.g. only one of 1, 3 and 3,1 may be written down. This will affect their table and patterns.

Number of jumpers	2	3	4	5
Ways to share them	3	4	5	6

Your child should notice that both patterns go up in 1s and that the number of ways to share the jumpers is always one more than how many jumpers there are. Use this knowledge to predict other answers (and then get your child to test them out!).

M1

Each of the eight pieces of the EIGHT–piece bar must be kept whole. Be systematic and spot patterns to find all the possible solutions.

1)

General	1	2	3	4	5	6	7
Ivor	7	6	5	4	3	2	1

2) 28 ways

General	Ivor	Mouse
6	1	1
5	2	1
5	1	2
4	3	1
4	1	3
4	2	2
3	1	4

General	Ivor	Mouse
3	4	1
3	2	3
3	3	2
6	1	1
5	2	1
5	1	2
4	3	1

General	Ivor	Mouse
4	1	3
4	2	2
3	1	4
3	4	1
3	2	3
3	3	2
2	4	2

General	Ivor	Mouse
2	3	3
1	6	1
1	1	6
1	5	2
1	2	5
1	4	3
1	3	4

Da Vinci files

Ivor	General	Mouse	Goat
5	1	1	1
4	1	1	2
4	1	2	1
4	2	1	1

Ivor	General	Mouse	Goat
4	2	1	1
3	2	1	2
3	2	1	2
3	1	2	2

TM

1) A plays B   A plays C   A plays D   B plays C   B plays D   C plays D   6 matches (3 + 2 + 1)
2) 3 x 20 mins = 60mins = 1 hour   So 6 x 20mins = 2 hours

M1   Be systematic. Use a table to help you find all the possible solutions.

1) (6 solutions)

Team A	0	0	0	1	1	1
Team B	0	1	2	0	1	2

2) (12 solutions)

Team C	0	0	0	0	1	1	1	1	2	2	2	2
Team D	0	1	2	3	0	1	2	3	0	1	2	3

3) (10 solutions)

Team B	0	0	1	1	2	2	3	3	4	4
Team D	0	1	0	1	0	1	0	1	0	1

Da Vinci files

Look at M1. Give each score a value (£3 per goal).
There must be 9 goals scored at half time (£3 x 9 = £27).
Work through the matches for combinations that have 9 goals.

Using the answers to M1 there are 70 possible combinations of scores, e.g. the three pairs of scores could be (0,1), (0,3), (4,1). In order to ensure all possible combinations are obtained a systematic listing needs to be used.

TM

1)

1st carriage	R	R	B	B
2nd carriage	R	B	R	B

There are 2 colour choices for the first carriage and 2 colour choices for the second carriage. 2 x 2 = 4 different combinations.

2)

1st carriage	R	R	R	B	R	B	B	B
2nd carriage	R	R	B	R	B	R	B	B
3rd carriage	R	B	R	R	B	B	R	B

There are 2 colour choices for the first carriage, 2 colour choices for the second carriage and 2 colour choices for the third carriage. 2 x 2 x 2 = 8 diferent combinations.

M1

1)

1st carriage	R	R	R	R	B	R	R	R	B	B	B	R	B	B	B	B
2nd carriage	R	R	R	B	R	R	B	B	R	R	B	B	R	B	B	B
3rd carriage	R	R	B	R	R	B	R	B	R	B	B	B	R	R	B	B
4th carriage	R	B	R	R	R	B	B	R	B	R	R	B	B	B	R	B

There are 2 colour choices for the first carriage, 2 colour choices for the second carriage, 2 colour choices for the third carriage and 2 colour choices for the fourth carriage. 2 x 2 x 2 x 2 = 16 different combinations.

2)

1st carriage	R	R	B	B	R	G	G	B	G
2nd carriage	R	B	R	B	G	R	G	G	B

There are 3 colour choices for the first carriage and 3 colour choices for the second carriage. 3 x 3 = 9 different combinations.

Da Vinci files

There are 3 colour choices for the first carriage, 3 colour choices for the second carriage and 3 colour choices for the third carriage.
3 x 3 x 3 = 27 different combinations.

MISSION FILE 2:10 — A right spotty bunch!

TM

1)
4	2	4
0		3
6	1	3

ML

5 solutions. Need to use a systematic method using 1, 2, 3... in turn. Could start by putting 1 in the top left position and working clockwise around the table, then trying a new position and starting again.

1 4 5	2 4 4	3 4 3	4 4 2	5 4 1
7 3	6 3	5 3	4 3	3 3
2 6 2	2 5 3	2 4 4	2 3 5	2 2 6

Da Vinci Files

The number of spots on the patients on the top right hand chair and the bottom right hand chair only have one possible solution. Work these out first, then investigate how many spots could be on the patients sitting on the other chairs.

3 5 6 8	3 5 6 8	3 5 6 8	3 5 6 8
18 4	17 4	16 4	15 4
1 7 4 10	2 6 4 10	3 5 3 10	4 4 4 10

3 5 6 8	3 5 6 8	3 5 6 8
14 4	13 4	12 4
5 3 4 10	6 2 4 10	7 1 4 10

(7 possibilities)

MISSION FILE 2:11 — A peculiar planet

TM

1) 3 Zogs and 2 Zugs

2) 2 Zogs and 3 Zugs   or   5 Zogs and 1 Zug

ML

1) 3 Zogs and 3 Zugs

2) 3 Zogs and 7 Zugs   or   6 Zogs and 3 Zugs

Da Vinci Files

(4 solutions)

Zigs (5s)	Zogs (4s)	Zugs (3s)
4	1	1
2	2	3
1	1	6
1	4	2

MISSION FILE 2:12 — Tree planting!

TM

1) 12 trees
2) 3 rows
3)
Rows	1	2	3	4	6	8	12	24
Trees	24	12	8	6	4	3	2	1

ML

1) a) 1 on each vertex, 5 between each pair of vertices
    b) 6 along each side
2) a) 1 on each vertex, 3 between each pair of vertices
    b) 4 along each side

Da Vinci Files

There are 72 possible ways. Each of the following combinations can be permuted (rearranged) in 6 different ways amongst Echo, Summer, and Forrest:

2, 2, 20   2, 4, 18   2, 6, 16   2, 8, 14   2, 10, 12   4, 4, 16
4, 6, 14   4, 8, 12   4, 10, 10   6, 6, 12   6, 8, 10   8, 8, 8

12 × 6 = 72 ways

TM

1) and 2) 1,9   2,8   3,7   4,6   5,5   6,4   7,3   8,2   9,1   (9 ways)
NB: Your child may choose not to record both combinations for a particular split, e.g. only one of 1, 9 and 9, 1 may be written down. This is if the boats are considered identical.

M1

1) 3 instructions are needed.
   4 from the 5th boat into the 4th.   1 from the 1st boat into the 3rd.   2 from the 1st boat into the 3rd.
2) 3, 4, 5, 6, 7

Da Vinci files

2 big boats and 6 small boats   OR   5 big boats and 2 small boats

TM

1) 9, 8, 7, 6 or 5 bags of turkeys
   $2 + 3 = 5$ $3 + 4 = 7$
   $2 + 4 = 6$ $3 + 5 = 8$
   $2 + 5 = 7$ $4 + 5 = 9$

2) 12, 11, 10 or 9 bags of turkeys
   $2 + 3 + 4 = 9$ $2 + 4 + 5 = 11$
   $2 + 3 + 5 = 10$ $3 + 4 + 5 = 12$

M1

1) 7 and 3 or 5, 3 and 2. Two ways to make 10, so arrested either 2 or 3 agents.
2) 7 and 4 or 5, 4 and 2. Two ways to make 11, so arrested either 2 or 3 agents.
3) 7 and 5 or 7, 2 and 3 or 5, 4 and 3. Three ways to make 12, so arrested either 2 or 3 agents.

Da Vinci files

7, 4 and 2. One way to make 13 so 3 arrests.
7, 5 and 2 or 7, 3 and 4 or 5, 4, 2 and 3. Three ways to make 14 so 3 or 4 arrests.
7, 5 and 3. One way to make 15 so 3 arrests.
7, 5 and 4 or 7, 5, 3 and 2. Two ways to make 16 so 3 or 4 arrests.

Check your child is working with the rules established above.

TM

1) There are 12 possible sums.
   $2 + 3 = 5$ $3 + 2 = 5$ $4 + 2 = 6$ $2 + 4 = 6$
   $3 + 4 = 7$ $4 + 3 = 7$ $2 + 3 + 4 = 9$ $2 + 4 + 3 = 9$
   $3 + 2 + 4 = 9$ $3 + 4 + 2 = 9$ $4 + 2 + 3 = 9$ $4 + 3 + 2 = 9$
2) 4 different totals: 5, 6, 7, 9
3) There are 60 possible sums.
   N.B. Some children may not write down both of $2 + 3 = 5$ and $3 + 2 = 5$ etc, because they appreciate that addition is commutative.

M1

1)
   $2 + 2 = 4$ $3 + 2 = 5$ $4 + 2 = 6$ $5 + 2 = 7$ $6 + 2 = 8$ $8 + 2 = 10$
   $2 + 3 = 5$ $3 + 3 = 6$ $4 + 3 = 7$ $5 + 3 = 8$ $6 + 3 = 9$ $8 + 3 = 11$
   $2 + 4 = 6$ $3 + 4 = 7$ $4 + 4 = 8$ $5 + 4 = 9$ $6 + 4 = 10$ $8 + 4 = 12$
   $2 + 5 = 7$ $3 + 5 = 8$ $4 + 5 = 9$ $5 + 5 = 10$ $6 + 5 = 11$ $8 + 5 = 13$
   $2 + 6 = 8$ $3 + 6 = 9$ $4 + 6 = 10$ $5 + 6 = 11$ $6 + 6 = 12$ $8 + 6 = 14$
   $2 + 8 = 10$ $3 + 8 = 11$ $4 + 8 = 12$ $5 + 8 = 13$ $6 + 8 = 14$ $8 + 8 = 16$
   $6 \times 6 = 36$ sums. You have 6 choices for your first number and 6 choices for your second number, excluding zero. If zero is included, you have 7 choices for the first number and 7 choices for the second number, $7 \times 7 = 49$ possible sums, 36 as above and $0 + 0 = 0$
   $0 + 2 = 2$ $2 + 0 = 2$ $0 + 3 = 3$ $3 + 0 = 3$ $0 + 4 = 4$ $4 + 0 = 4$ $0 + 5 = 5$ $5 + 0 = 5$ $0 + 6 = 6$ $6 + 0 = 6$ $0 + 8 = 8$
   $8 + 0 = 8$
   N.B. Some children may not write down both of $2 + 3 = 5$ and $3 + 2 = 5$ etc, because they appreciate that addition is commutative.
2) There are 12 different totals: 4, 5, 6, 7, 8, 9, 10, 11, 12, 13, 14, 16. If zero is included, there are 15 different totals: 0, 2, 3, 4, 5, 6, 7, 8, 9, 10, 11, 12, 13, 14, 16.

1) For two different numbers there are 72 possible sums, 9 choices for the first number, 8 choices for the second, 9 x 8 = 72. See N.B. in TM as children may also appreciate that multiplication is commutative. Multiplying any number by zero results in the answer zero, so 0 on the calculator has not been used.

1 x 2 = 2	2 x 1 = 2	9 x 1 = 9
...	...	...
...	...	...
1 x 3 = 3	2 x 3 = 6	9 x 2 = 18
1 x 9 = 9	2 x 9 = 18	9 x 8 = 72

2) For three different numbers there will be 9 x 8 x 7 = 504 sums.
(If commutative property is appreciated then there will be $\frac{504}{6}$ = 84 sums.)

MISSION FILE 2:16   Echo is no birdbrain!

TM

1)

Uni (1)	Bi (2)	Tri (3)	Quad (4)
5	0	0	0
3	1	0	0
1	2	0	0
2	0	1	0
0	1	1	0
1	0	0	1

2) 6 ways

MI

1)

Uni (1)	Bi (2)	Tri (3)	Quad (4)
6	0	0	0
4	1	0	0
3	0	1	0
2	2	0	0
2	0	0	1
1	1	1	0
0	3	0	0
0	1	0	1
0	0	2	0

2) 9 possibilities

Da Vinci files

Uni (1)	Bi (2)	Tri (3)	Quad (4)
7	0	0	0
5	1	0	0
4	0	1	0
3	2	0	0
3	0	0	1
2	1	1	0
1	3	0	0
0	0	1	1
1	0	2	0
1	1	0	1

MISSION FILE 2:17   A tiring investigation

TM

The area outside the circles could be counted as a region too. Add 1 to each solution if required for all questions.

1) 2 areas   (1) (2)   2) 3 areas   (1(2)3)

MF1

1) 7 areas

2) 13 areas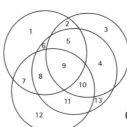

Other solutions may be possible.

Da Vinci Files

£5 x 21 = £105

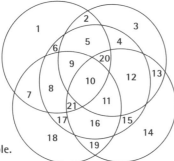

Other solutions may be possible.

MISSION FILE 2:18 — Victor's key to success

TM

1) (1, 2) (1, 3) (1, 4)
   (2, 3) (2, 4)
   (3, 4)
   6 ways = 3 + 2 + 1

2) (1, 2, 3) (1, 2, 4)
   (1, 3, 4)
   (2, 3, 4)
   4 ways = 2 + 1 + 1

3) (1, 2, 3, 4)
   1 way

MF1

1) (1, 2) (1, 3) (1, 4) (1, 5) (1, 6) (1, 7) (1, 8) (1, 9)   8
   (2, 3) (2, 4) (2, 5) (2, 6) (2, 7) (2, 8) (2, 9)   7
   (3, 4) (3, 5) (3, 6) (3, 7) (3, 8) (3, 9)   6
   (4, 5) (4, 6) (4, 7) (4, 8) (4, 9)   5
   (5, 6) (5, 7) (5, 8) (5, 9)   4
   (6, 7) (6, 8) (6, 9)   3
   (7, 8) (7, 9)   2
   (8, 9)   1

   8 + 7 + 6 + 5 + 4 + 3 + 2 + 1 = 36 combinations

2) (1, 2, 3) (1, 2, 4) (1, 2, 5) (1, 2, 6) (1, 2, 7) (1, 2, 8) (1, 2, 9)   7
   (1, 3, 4) (1, 3, 5) (1, 3, 6) (1, 3, 7) (1, 3, 8) (1, 3, 9)   6
   (1, 4, 5) (1, 4, 6) (1, 4, 7) (1, 4, 8) (1, 4, 9)   5
   (1, 5, 6) (1, 5, 7) (1, 5, 8) (1, 5, 9)   4
   (1, 6, 7) (1, 6, 8) (1, 6, 9)   3
   (1, 7, 8) (1, 7, 9)   2
   (1, 8, 9)   1

   (2, 3, 4) (2, 3, 5) (2, 3, 6) (2, 3, 7) (2, 3, 8) (2, 3, 9)   6
   (2, 4, 5) (2, 4, 6) (2, 4, 7) (2, 4, 8) (2, 4, 9)   5
   (2, 5, 6) (2, 5, 7) (2, 5, 8) (2, 5, 9)   4
   (2, 6, 7) (2, 6, 8) (2, 6, 9)   3
   (2, 7, 8) (2, 7, 9)   2
   (2, 8, 9)   1

   and so on.

   (7 + 6 + 5 + 4 + 3 + 2 + 1) + (6 + 5 + 4 + 3 + 2 + 1) + (5 + 4 + 3 + 2 + 1) + (4 + 3 + 2 + 1) + (3 + 2 + 1) + (2 + 1) + (1) = 84 combinations

   OR (7 x 1) + (6 x 2) + (5 x 3) + (4 x 4) + (3 x 5) + (2 x 6) + (1 x 7) = 84

Da Vinci Files

6 + 5 + 4 + 3 + 2 + 1 = 21 which corresponds to 7 buttons.

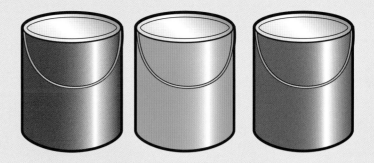

Answering these questions will mean that painting can begin. It may even be dry by next Tuesday!

1) How many ways are there that Victor can paint FOUR carriages using the tins of red and blue paint?

2) Victor wants to use green paint as well. How many ways are there that Victor can paint TWO carriages using the THREE different colours?

Completing the Da Vinci Challenge will ensure that a very colourful train will be charging along the tracks in no time.

Da Vinci files

Victor has red, blue and green paint.

Try finding different ways that THREE carriages can be painted using some or all of the tins of paint.

Huxley's Think Tank

Try using squared paper and colour pencils to record your work. You could try writing a letter to stand for each of the colours.

A right spotty bunch!

Time: Early evening
Place: Breakneck Hospital

Doctors at Breakneck Hospital are unable to cure the very contagious disease 'Turkey Pox'. Prince Barrington has agreed to help. He thinks that as long as it is known how many spots each sufferer has, they can be cured in no time.

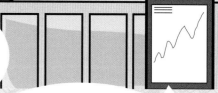

Where shall I start, Da Vinci?

Huxley has a Training Mission to test this idea of yours!

Prince Barrington invites the sufferers to sit around a square table. They must sit so that the number of spots of the people on each side add up to the same number.

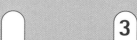

4 2

3

1

The patients sit around the table so that the number of spots on each side of the table adds up to 10.

Fill up the empty chairs by working out how many spots a person would need to have to sit on it.

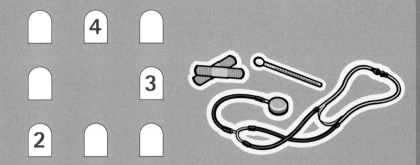

The nurses and doctors notice that some of the patients' spots seem to be vanishing! They race off to get some more sufferers to bring to Prince Barrington. Each of the patients has at least ONE spot.

The patients sit around the table so that the number of spots on each side of the table adds up to TEN.

Fill up the empty chairs by working out how many spots a person would need to have to sit on it.

Investigate how many ways there are to do this.

Congratulations! Sitting round a table in this way really does seem to cure people! Completing the Da Vinci Challenge will ensure that there are no spotty sufferers in the hospital at all!

Da Vinci files

The number of spots along each side of this rectangular table adds up to 22. Investigate how many spots could be on the patients sitting on the empty chairs. Each patient has at least ONE spot.

Huxley's Think Tank

Draw the spots to help you work out the answers. Check your additions by using subtraction.

A peculiar planet!

Time: Midnight
Place: Planet Craggy

Victor Blastov has just landed his spaceship on Planet Craggy. He has come to investigate rumours that there are some strange aliens living here. Victor Blastov needs to count these crazy creatures. The problem is the Zogs and Zugs are so excited to see him that they just won't stay still. This is a job for Brain Academy!

These critters von't stop vriggling! Vot do I do, Da Vinci?

Once you've done the Huxley's Training Mission you'll be counting aliens in no time!

TM

Victor will need your help to count the first gang of aliens. You'll need to remember that Zogs have TWO arms and Zugs have THREE arms.

Victor sees a group of aliens, which have a total of 12 arms. There is at least ONE Zog and ONE Zug in the group.

1) How many Zogs and Zugs does he see?

2) How many Zogs are there if there is a total of 13 arms with at least ONE Zog and ONE Zug? Find both solutions.

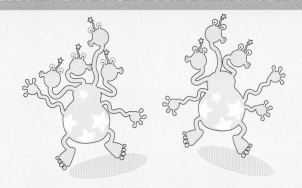

Victor needs to count some other groups of aliens which are still going crazy on Craggy. If you're going to help Victor, you'll need to remember that Zogs have FOUR heads and Zugs have THREE heads.

Victor knows there is at least ONE Zog and ONE Zug. He counts 21 heads.

1) How many Zogs and Zugs are there?

Victor counts 33 heads.

2) How many Zogs and Zugs could he see?
How many solutions can you find?

Keeping track of all the Zogs and Zugs is enough to make Victor's head spin! The Da Vinci Challenge below will make him an alien counting champion!

Da Vinci files

A new alien appears on Planet Craggy called a Zig. It has FIVE heads!

There is at least ONE of each alien in view all the time. If Victor can see 27 heads how many Zigs, Zogs and Zugs could there be?

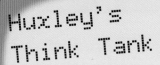

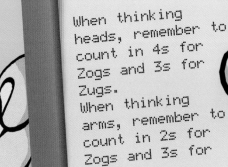

Huxley's Think Tank

When thinking heads, remember to count in 4s for Zogs and 3s for Zugs.
When thinking arms, remember to count in 2s for Zogs and 3s for Zugs.

Tree planting!

Time: Early morning
Place: Trunkton village

A terrible hurricane has blown down a large number of beautiful trees in Trunkton village. Echo the Eco-Warrior, along with two of her friends, has agreed to lend a hand and help plant 24 new trees in the village. Can you help Echo and her pals restore the village to how it used to be?

Da Vinci? What shall we do?

Put on your wellies and get ready for your Training Mission!

TM

Before Echo and her friends begin planting, they need to dig holes for 24 trees.

1) Echo wants to plant the trees in TWO equal rows. How many holes do they need to dig in each row?

2) Her friends want to plant EIGHT trees in each row. How many rows do they need?

3) Find all the ways they could plant the trees in rows so that there are the same number of trees in each row and none left over.

M1

The THREE friends are ready to begin planting those trees. Answer these questions to start restoring this empty village.

On Monday morning, the three friends plant 24 trees, splitting them equally between the sides of a SQUARE. They plant a tree on each vertex.

1) How many do they plant along each side?

2) How many would they plant on each side if they didn't plant a tree in each corner?

On Monday afternoon, the friends planted another 24 trees splitting them equally between the sides of a HEXAGON. They plant a tree on each vertex.

3) How many do they plant along each side?

4) How many would they plant on each side if they didn't plant a tree in each corner?

Wow, the village is looking great! Completing the Da Vinci Challenge will ensure those final trees get planted!

Da Vinci Files

On Monday evening, the three friends, Echo, Summer and Forest, plant another 24 trees. Each friend plants an even number of trees.

Find all the different ways that they could do this.

Huxley's Think Tank

Remember: a corner of a shape is called a vertex.

Man overboard!

Time: Early afternoon
Place: A beach in Spain

Prince Barrington is lying on the beach, enjoying his summer holiday, when he notices a problem. A dinghy full of people is being swept out to sea. Prince Barrington knows he must save these people, but how?

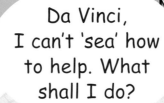

Da Vinci, I can't 'sea' how to help. What shall I do?

Huxley's Training Mission should help you save the day.

TM

If Prince Barrington can complete the Training Mission, the lifeboat will soon be on its way.

TEN lifeboat people climb into TWO boats. How many people could there be in each boat?

Find all the possible answers. There must be at least ONE person in each boat.

Lifeboat men are sent out to rescue the people. They go in FIVE boats. There should be an equal number of men in each boat, but in their hurry some get in the wrong boats.

1) What is the minimum number of instructions that the Prince must give so that there are an equal number of people in each boat? What are these instructions?

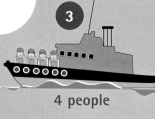
1
8 people

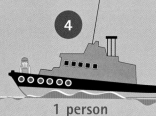
2
3 people

3
4 people

4
1 person

5
9 people

2) The Prince then decides to rearrange these people so that each boat in the line has ONE more person than the last. How many people will there be in each boat?

If the Prince can complete the Da Vinci Challenge, the lifeboat men will return the people safely to the shore.

Da Vinci files

There are 26 people in some lifeboats, which are full.
A big lifeboat holds FOUR people.
A small lifeboat holds THREE people.

How many big and small boats could there be?
There are TWO possible answers.
Can you find them both?

Huxley's Think Tank

Using cubes or counters may help you.

A 'foul' act

Time: December, early one morning
Place: Buster Crimes' police station

A group of evil D.A.F.T. agents have decided to try to spoil Christmas celebrations by breaking into shops and stealing all the frozen turkeys. Buster Crimes knows that it is his job to catch the agents and save Christmas!

This is a 'foul' act Da Vinci! How do I solve this crime?

'Yule' need to start with Huxley's Training Mission.

To make sure there's turkey on everyone's plate this Christmas, Crimes will need to arrest those thieves. Can you help him by answering these questions?'

1) Crimes arrests TWO D.A.F.T. agents. How many sacks of turkeys could they have between them?

2) How many sacks of turkeys could THREE D.A.F.T. agents have between them?

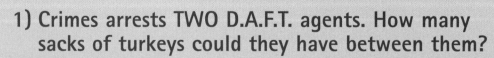

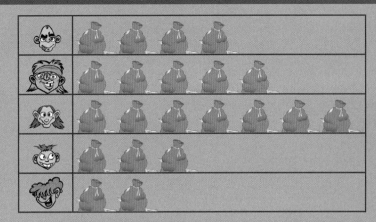

Crimes wants to send these D.A.F.T. agents to prison, where they belong. Help him to do this by answering these questions.

1) Crimes arrests some D.A.F.T. agents. Altogether they have 10 sacks of turkeys. How many agents did he arrest? Is there more than one possible answer?

2) What if the agents have 11 sacks of turkeys? How many agents did he arrest? Is there more than one possible answer?

3) If there is a total of 12 sacks, how many arrests has he made? How many possible answers are there?

Completing the Da Vinci Challenge will mean that the turkeys can be stuffed and people can feel stuffed!

Da Vinci Files

Investigate the possible number of arrests that Crimes could have made if there was a total of 13, 14, 15 and 16 sacks of turkeys. Don't forget that there may be more than one answer.

Huxley's Think Tank

Draw pictures of the sacks to help you. Work through each combination step by step.

5, 4, 3, 2, 1 BLASTOV!

Time: 4.50pm
Place: NASA headquarters

Victor Blastov is trying to programme his rocket to fly to Mars. He needs to do some very difficult sums but his calculator just won't work properly! Time to call Brain Academy!

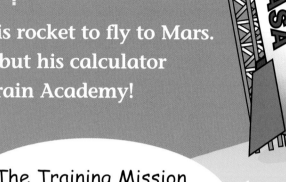

Vot should I do, Da Vinci?

The Training Mission that Huxley has for you will get you off to a flying start!

Can you help Victor to program his rocket by answering these questions?

1) By using each of the numbers TWO, THREE and FOUR no more than once, write down as many addition sums as you can find.

2) How many different totals are there?

3) Now include the number FIVE. How many sums can you find?

Answering these questions will mean that Victor can begin his journey to Mars. Remember, numbers ONE, SEVEN and NINE are broken on his calculator, so can't be used.

1) Pick a pair of numbers and using only the + sign write as many different sums as you can find.

2) How many different totals are there?

Excellent! All that button pressing has made the calculator work! Completing the Da Vinci Challenge will allow Victor to land safely on Mars!

Da Vinci files

The calculator is now working.

1) Using any TWO numbers and the x sign write as many different sums as you can find.

2) Now investigate with THREE numbers.

Huxley's Think Tank

Answers that are the same can be made using different sums.

Remember
$3+2=5$ $2+3=5$
$3-2=1$ $3-1=2$

Echo is no birdbrain!

tri

quad

bi

uni

Time: Just after lunch
Place: A park in South London

A flock of South American Fluffy-Nuts has escaped from the 'American National Zoo' and headed straight for England. Each bird has its own unique colour of crest feathers. Echo has agreed to help return these rare and beautiful birds. She needs to call Brain Academy...

Da Vinci? What must I do?

Get your coat and get ready for your training mission with Huxley

OK Echo. First you must take photographs of the birds so that the zookeeper can identify them.

1) In the first phototograph there are five different crest feathers. Which birds could have been in the photograph?

2) How many possible answers can you find?

Echo needs to take photographs of all the birds to send to the zookeeper. Answer these questions and he'll be sure to recognise them.

1) In the next photograph there are six different crest feathers. Which birds could be in the photograph?

2) How many different answers can you find?

Fantastic! The zookeeper has identified his birds. If Echo can take the Da Vinci Challenge she can return them to their home.

Da Vinci files

In the next photograph, Echo sees SEVEN different crest feathers. Which birds could be in the photograph?

Huxley's Think Tank

Write the names and number of feathers at the top of your page.
Work out sums using the lowest numbers first.

A tiRING investigation!

Time: Past midnight
Place: A jewellery store

An evil D.A.F.T. agent, Mrs I Steal, has broken into a jewellery store and stolen some expensive gold rings. Buster Crimes is desperate to catch this wicked woman. He needs to 'ring' Brain Academy.

What must I do Da Vinci?

Huxley has a golden Training Mission planned for you.

TM

As Mrs Steal is running out of the shop, she drops TWO gold rings on the floor. To complete your Training Mission you need to find how many areas the rings made as they fell in a pile on the floor.

1) What is the least number of areas that the TWO rings could make as they land on the floor? Don't forget that they are all the same size and they don't have to overlap.

2) What is the greatest number of areas that TWO rings could form as they fall on the floor?

Answering these questions will mean that Mrs I Steal will be put behind bars. (Not gold bars though!) Can you help Buster by counting the areas that these rings form as they fall on the floor?

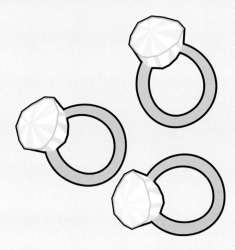

1) What is the greatest number of areas that THREE rings can form as they land on the floor?

2) How about the greatest number of areas for FOUR rings?

Completing the Da Vinci Challenge will mean that Buster will be able to return the gold rings to the shop.

REWARD

Da Vinci files

A reward is offered for the return of the rings. Five rings were stolen. If £5 is offered for each area made, how much is the largest reward that could be paid?

Huxley's Think Tank

An area is a marked out space where the rings can fall. Where two rings fall on the floor and overlap an extra area is formed. Try using some hoops to test this out.

Victor's key to success

Time: Past bedtime
Place: Space Research Lab

Victor Blastov is playing with his new computer. He's trying
to make it work with the lights ON and the sound OFF,
so he can beat his best ever score at 'Space Wars'.
He needs to call Brain Academy...

Da Vinci?
Vot must I do?

Press the ON button and
get ready for your Training
Mission with Huxley.

TM

Victor's computer
has FOUR keys. If he solves this
Training Mission the lights on his
computer will come ON.

1) How many different ways can
TWO keys be pressed together?

2) Now try with THREE keys.

3) How about FOUR keys?

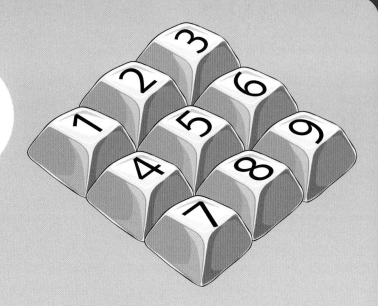

M1

Victor has to upgrade his computer to play the game. It now has NINE keys. Answer these questions so Victor can turn the sound OFF.

1) How many combinations are there if TWO keys are pressed?

2) Now try with THREE keys.

MISSION COMPLETE! With the lights ON and the sound OFF, Victor can now try to beat his hi-score on 'Space Wars'.

Da Vinci files

On one of Victor's old computers, if he pressed two keys together he had 21 combinations. How many keys did Victor's old computer have?

Huxley's Think Tank

Look for patterns in your work.

Mission Strategies 1

Use the TASC Problem-solving Wheel to guide you through the Mission Files. It will help you to become more confident and think of ideas for yourself. You might find it helpful to start at *Gather/organise* and work clockwise around the Wheel using the questions to help you think through each problem.

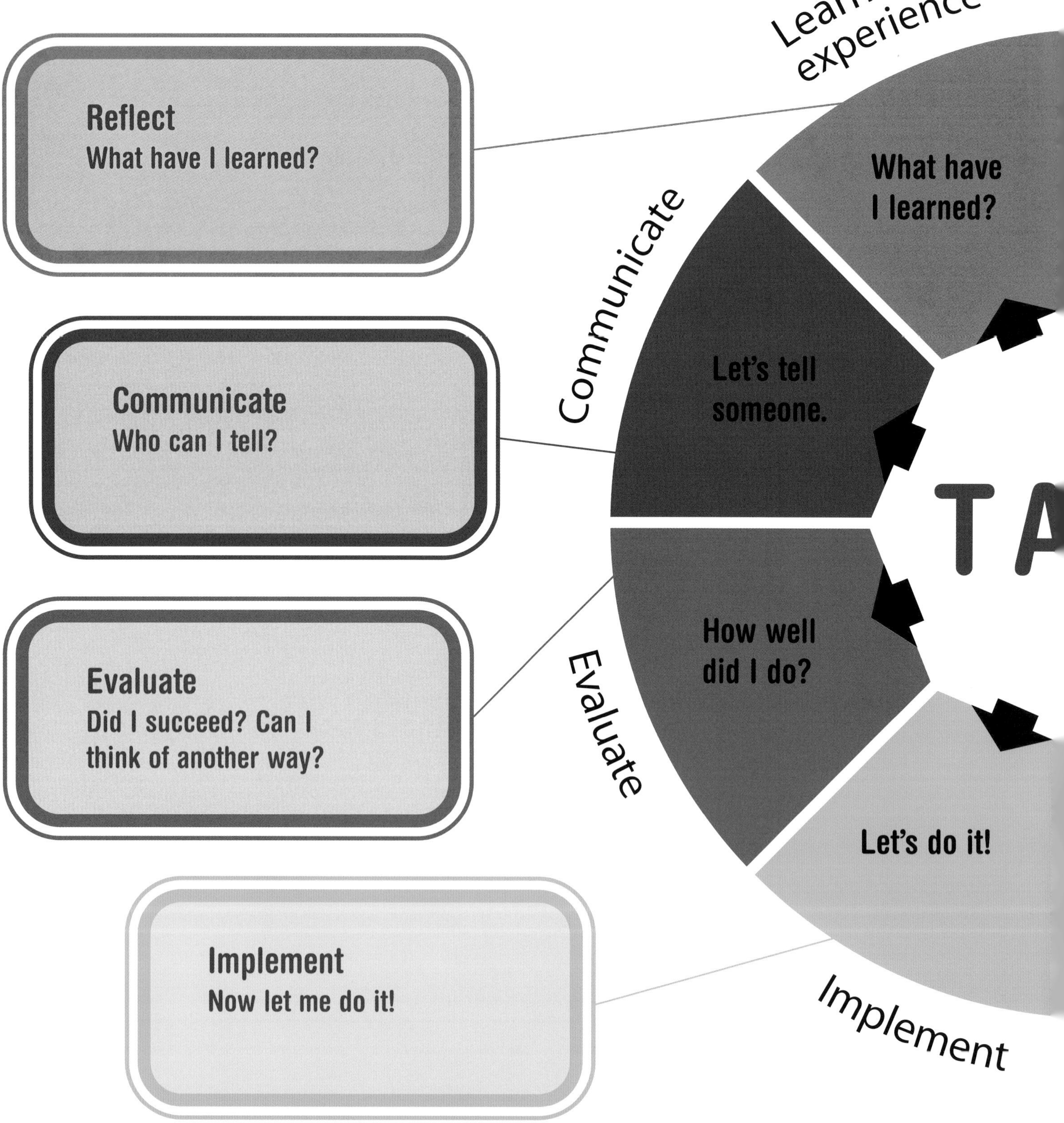

Learn from experience

Communicate

Reflect
What have I learned?

Communicate
Who can I tell?

Evaluate
Did I succeed? Can I think of another way?

Implement
Now let me do it!

What have I learned?

Let's tell someone.

Evaluate

How well did I do?

TA

Let's do it!

Implement

We can learn to be expert thinkers!

Gather/organise

What do I know about this?

Identify

What is the task?

S C

Generate

How many ideas can I think of?

Which is the best idea?

Decide

Gather and Organise
What do I already know about this?

Identify
What am I trying to do?

Generate
How many ways can I do this?

Decide
Which is the best way?

TASC: Thinking Actively in a Social Context © Belle Wallace 2004

MISSION FILE 2:1
Always start with the lowest value coin – 1p – and try to make each amount with just 1p pieces first. Then change two 1ps for a 2p and so on through the missions.

MISSION FILE 2:2
Put a mirror in the middle of your symmetrical pattern. You should see the same beads in the mirror that are on the other side of your design.

MISSION FILE 2:3
Identify what you are trying to do. Are you looking for the number of coins or an amount of money?

MISSION FILE 2:4
Work out the pattern for the first question, then try it out on the rest of the questions. This is a quick and simple way of completing this Mission!

MISSION FILE 2:5
Try different combinations here. Think about what you know – dogs have four legs and officers have two legs. You also know the number of legs in total!

MISSION FILE 2:6
For the Da Vinci File try listing the different scores in a step-by-step way, starting with $1 + 1 + 1 = 3$ and moving up to $1 + 1 + 2$ and so on.

MISSION FILE 2:7
When you have noticed the rules about the numbers, write them down and remember to use them again.

MISSION FILE 2:8
Start the Mission File 1 with a 0–0 score and move on from there. Are there any other ways you can find of doing this activity?

MISSION FILE 2:9
Can you see any patterns in your answers? Clue: They relate to the number of carriages that are painted!

MISSION FILE 2:10
You need to think step–by–step here. Start by putting 1 in the top left position, 2 in the top centre position and 3 in the top right position. Now work clockwise round the table. Then try a new starting position and begin again.

MISSION FILE 2:11
What do you know about these questions? The answers are all about the number of arms and heads, so write down the information you have been given first.

MISSION FILE 2:12
A vertex is a corner. Think about what you know about the numbers of corners in a square or hexagon.

MISSION FILE 2:13
In the Da Vinci File decide the best way to solve the problem and then use this way to find BOTH possible answers.

MISSION FILE 2:14
Start by adding two bags and three bags to get five bags. Then add two bags to four bags and so on.

MISSION FILE 2:15
Use what you know from the Training Mission to start your solution to Mission 1, then look at what other ways you need to find.

MISSION FILE 2:16
Write down what you know first. Then what you need to find out. Remember that the birds have their own UNIQUE set of coloured feathers.

MISSION FILE 2:17
Draw each of the different regions first. These are a bit like VENN DIAGRAMS. Remember, sometimes the two rings won't touch!

MISSION FILE 2:18
Look at the pattern in the Training Mission. This should help you solve the rest of the problems in Mission 1 and the Da Vinci Files.

nace●

What is NACE?

NACE is an independent charity set up in 1984. It supports the teaching of more able learners and helps all children to find out what they are good at and to do their best.

What does NACE do?

NACE helps teachers by giving them advice, books, materials and training. Many teachers, headteachers, parents and governors join NACE. The NACE website gives its members useful advice, ideas and materials to help children to learn.

How will this book help me?

The Brain Academy Maths books challenge and help you to become better at learning and a better mathematician by:
- thinking of and testing different solutions to problems;
- making connections to what you already know;
- making mistakes and learning from them;
- working by yourself and with others;
- expecting you to get better and to go on to the next book;
- learning skills which you can use in other subjects and out of school.

We hope that you enjoy the books!

Rising Stars Ltd, 7 Hatchers Mews, Bermondsey Street, London SE1 3GS